BLACKPOOL
THEN & NOW

IN COLOUR

JOHN BURKE

The
History
Press

To Frances, with my love and thanks.

First published in 2013

The History Press
The Mill, Brimscombe Port
Stroud, Gloucestershire, GL5 2QG
www.thehistorypress.co.uk

© John Burke, 2013

British Library Cataloguing in Publication Data.
A catalogue record for this book is available from the British Library.

ISBN 978 0 7524 8616 1

Typesetting and origination by The History Press
Printed in India.

CONTENTS

ACKNOWLEDGEMENTS

I am indebted to the following individuals and organisations:

Mr Chris Wynne of Shrewsbury for the kind loan of postcards featured on the following pages: 8, 16, 22, 33, 34, 62, 65, 74, 78, 83, 85 and 86.

The Local and Family History Centre at Blackpool Central Library for permission to reproduce postcards and photographs on pages 48, 51 and 56.

For access to premises to gain viewpoints to take the modern-day photographs, my thanks go to: Nick Hyde, PR & Marketing Dept of Blackpool Pleasure Beach; Anne Houghton, Tommy Ducks pub and restaurant, South Promenade; South Pier; the proprietors, Regency Holiday Flats, South Promenade; Central Pier; the proprietors and manager, Central Beach Holiday Flats, Central Promenade; Stephen Mercer, North Pier; the manager and staff, Blackpool Central Travelodge, Talbot Square; the manager and staff, Belvedere Hotel, the Gynn.

All other postcard views and all present-day photographs are from the author's collection.
I should like to thank my ever-supportive family, particularly my wife, Fran, for her encouragement and understanding, particularly on those days when the sun came out for five minutes as she was serving a meal, only for me to grab a camera and dash out!

ABOUT THE AUTHOR

John Burke started his career as a professional photographer and has written and illustrated articles for numerous local and national magazines and websites, both in the UK and abroad.

An ex-President of the Blackpool and Fylde Photographic Society, John's photographs have been used in books, magazines and exhibited in art galleries.

INTRODUCTION

Blackpool is England's – nay, the UK's and arguably Europe's – best-known seaside resort. Rising from obscurity not much more than 150 years ago, Blackpool nonetheless has an impressive record of innovation, world firsts, development and progress – after all, 'Progress' is the town's motto.

The first electric street tramway opened in 1885, and Blackpool is the only town in England to have continuously operated a tramway since that time to the present day. The first electric street lamps were switched on here, starting a tradition of lighting displays that came to be the world-famous Blackpool Illuminations.

Blackpool Tower was originally only one of several mooted seaside towers. For a number of years there was one at New Brighton on the south side of the River Mersey, close enough for Morse messages to be sent between the two by flashing light.

The Pleasure Beach is another world-renowned company. It has been family owned since its early days and has one ride – Sir Hiram Maxim's Flying Machine – which has passed its centenary, yet it is still drawing riders today.

As 'Progress' is the town's motto there is plenty of evidence of it in this book. Recently the Promenade has been subject to a massive redevelopment to both refurbish the sea defences and to modernise the look and feel of Blackpool. Such has been the scale of the work that it has altered the shape of Blackpool's coastline and extended it out to the west, reclaiming land from the sea.

For some of the photographs the actual scene has changed many times during the intervening period and some readers will remember other scenes, buildings or attractions that have come and gone in the years between 'then' and 'now'.

Whilst concentrating on the journey from south to north along the Promenade, the book takes a look around the town itself, following the long-disappeared tracks of the Circular Tour by tram, taking in the town centre and a look along one of the main routes into and out of the town.

The hotels of Blackpool are one reason behind its success as a holiday resort. We shall see them with gardens before the growing numbers of motor cars led to pressure for these green spaces to be turned into car-parking space. And we shall briefly remember the joys of staying in hotels in Blackpool's early days – with free use of the cruet...

We will be able to see how Blackpool developed and grew, expanding both north and south from a tiny central spot between the North Pier and Tower sites and towards earlier villages such as Bispham and Layton that are now overtaken by Blackpool.

Blackpool is still in the throes of progress. What wonders and what new sights will come and go over the next 100 years? Perhaps my great-great-grandson will write *that* book!

John D. Burke, 2012

THE DEEP SOUTH

BLACKPOOL WAS DEVELOPED around the area where the North Pier can be found and spread slowly in all directions except the west, where the Irish Sea gets in the way. Therefore the Edwardians made few postcards of the area south of the Pleasure Beach – apart from sand, there was nothing there.

This view is of the rockeries and landscaping of the 1920s, with the 'balloon' tram showing that the photograph was taken in the 1930s. The hotels are arranged in a crescent behind more

gardens and the Pleasure Beach, as yet, has no rides tall enough to peep over the roof of the Starr Inn on the skyline (visible between the tram and the shelter).

The pier in the distance is the South Pier, of which we shall see more as we move northwards along the Promenade.

GONE ARE THE rockeries and the classical architecture of the shelters and sunken courtyards. A multi-level series of Promenades take their place in this 2012 view. Sinuous curves of railings (and in the layout of different coloured paving stones) are reflected even in the benches provided for strollers to take a rest. A series of artworks are exhibited from Squires Gate to the Pleasure Beach, and it was the first part of the Promenade to be redeveloped (although the old sea wall has been retained).

Further afield, the Pleasure Beach is now very evident with the red and blue steelwork of the Big One roller coaster reaching into the sky beyond the Starr Inn. On the South Pier, seen jutting out on the horizon to the left, the end-of-pier theatre buildings have gone and bungee towers and swings have taken their place.

THE PLEASURE BEACH

THE PLEASURE BEACH when new was aptly named. Before the extension of the Promenade Road, the attraction was built on the beach itself at the end of the road. The Pleasure Beach was established by Alderman William George Bean in 1896. Early rides included a bicycle railway and, from 1904, Hiram Maxim's Flying Machine, an attraction which still draws visitors to this day, over 100 years later.

By the time of our postcard in 1923 the Big Dipper has arrived but there is still no road, and no Promenade. On the beach nearby, a row of donkeys or ponies have their backs to us to keep their heads out of the wind whilst they wait for riders. In the 1930s the company passed into the ownership of the Thomson family – Leonard Thomson having married W.G. Bean's daughter, Doris. The Pleasure Beach is still owned by the Thomsons today.

THE BEACH TODAY has been driven back many yards away from its 1923 position. Two other roller coasters, the Big One and the Infusion, the roadway, the tramway, a large car park and then a wide Promenade all sit between the Big Dipper and the sand. The Big Dipper, brand new in 1923, is no longer at the very front of the park. A lake was created adjacent to the Big Dipper. In 1934 the actress Marlene Dietrich lost a pearl earring whilst riding this attraction. In 2007, when the lake was drained to build a new ride, the earring was found. A row of shops – Ocean Boulevard – has been built along the front of the Pleasure Beach.

9

THE CASINO BUILDING

THIS SPECTACULAR BUILDING was built in 1913. Described variously as being like an Indian palace or a wedding cake, the name 'casino' is not quite an apt description, as gambling was never allowed here. The flamboyant building housed restaurants and other catering outlets and was extravagantly lit at night. It gave the Pleasure Beach an instantly recognisable landmark, something to fix on whilst walking south down the Promenade. The arched windows down the side are matched by the arches of the grand entrance porch. It was to last only a single generation.

THE CURRENT BUILDING was designed as part of a large refurbishment of the park by architect Joseph Emberton in the late 1930s. The circular building provides a spectacular precursor to the Pleasure

Beach itself, with a bright red funnel adding a nautical element. At the rear is a glass tower containing a spiral staircase. The entrance is flanked by a square tower and a thin concrete spiral staircase and at night the building, like its predecessor, makes a spectacular addition to the town's famous Illuminations.

The interior includes a manager's suite of rooms with built-in furniture in art-deco style. For a period the building was renamed the Wonderful World building and housed a ride which took visitors, sitting in a suspended seat, around a series of animated tableaux featuring the world of entertainment. This was moved in the 1990s and the building reverted to its original name.

TOWARDS THE VICTORIA PIER

WE KNOW IT today as the South Pier. The last of Blackpool's three piers to be built, it opened on Good Friday, 1893. The Grand Pavilion at its end held 3,000 people. The massive Dreadnought trams were effective people-movers. The tracks opposite the Pleasure Beach, which is just behind this viewpoint, allowed four trams to wait side by side and pick up passengers.

In front of the Dreadnought on the left is a 'toast-rack' open-air tramcar. Basically just a moving platform with seats, the conductor swung himself from row to row down the side to collect fares.

The horse of the leading landau in the queue is gazing at the motor car, whose driver seems to be kneeling to fix some problem.

THE UNINTERRUPTED VISTA of beach and sea has gone. It went in the 1930s with the building of the open-air baths, themselves demolished during the 1980s to make way for the Sandcastle indoor pool complex, whose water slides we can see on the left. The northern part of the building is a casino.

The two gardens remain and we can see a little more of them in this view. The older photograph was taken from the old casino, which was rectangular. The new circular building has no viewpoints from nearer the roadway so we are looking from its roof balcony over the side of the garden nearest to us. It has a modern crazy-golf course. The one closer to the pier – which used to have nothing scarier than a tall flag mast – now houses a ghost train.

SOUTH OF THE PIER

A POSTCARD FROM the late Victorian era. The Big Wheel, seen on the skyline, was built in 1896. The tram has no pole and there are no wires overhead. The original 1885 tramway used a conduit system. The trams picked up electricity from a central slot, like toy racing cars. Sand blowing into the slot caused frequent shorts and breakdowns and there are tales of sheets of flame shooting up from the slot – which, whilst spectacular, may have concerned the operators even in those pre-health and safety conscious days! The trams converted to overhead lines in 1897 – giving a short time window for the photograph to have been taken.

On the right of the photograph is a vicarage with pretty gable ends. Note also the lack of any railings between the Promenade and the slope of the sea wall.

THE ENTRANCE TO the pier is fronted by a large amusements arcade to draw people in once the original novelty of walking over the water has lost its appeal. The Beachcomber Arcade was opened in 1963 following the conversion of a theatre, and for a long time the centrepiece of its attractions was a life-sized robot western gunslinger against which players drew a six gun.

The pier entrance is flanked on both sides by stalls selling ice-cream, kiss-me-quick hats, beach balls and various other items. Across the road, the gables of the old vicarage are still recognisable and for over half a century have covered Pablo's fish and chip restaurant where, in the 1960s, you could eat fish and chips with bread and butter and a pot of tea for *2s 6d*!

THE VICTORIA
(SOUTH) PIER

THE VICTORIA PIER got its name because when it was built Blackpool already had a North Pier and a South Pier – which we know today as the Central Pier. You can imagine the reluctance of the existing pier to change, even if a new pier further to the south made a mockery of its name. In order not to have to name the new pier 'The Even-Further-South Pier', the Victorians named it after their Queen.

It was the shortest but widest of the three piers, built so to cater for the swift passage of customers to the massive Grand Pavilion at its end.

The postcard company's artist has dropped in a blue sky with clouds, but has managed to create twin horizons with a slightly bizarre apparent 'hill' in the sea behind the pier!

TODAY'S SOUTH PIER has survived a number of fires but only with the loss of the end-of-the-pier theatre. This space has been utilised to house a small number of white-knuckle rides including a swing that sends its rider flying out over the side of the pier and a reverse bungee ride where riders are catapulted up into the air.

The twenty-first-century Promenade refurbishment has extended the Promenade out over what was previously beach. Walking over the waves these days would involve a shorter walk than in the early days of the pier!

SOUTH PROMENADE

IN THIS VIEW, looking north from the South Pier, the beach and sea wall appear as they would all the way from the early 1900s through to the recent Promenade refurbishment and development from 2007. People are taking advantage of the low tide to walk along the beach and a few families are playing in the drier sand around the Promenade steps. Blackpool's tide covers the sands entirely twice a day. This makes for an extremely good consistency of sand, allowing it to be modelled and shaped without immediately crumbling into coarse powder.

On the far side of the road the hotels have neat gardens adjoining the roadway, which carries very little traffic.

HAD WE TAKEN the photograph from the very same spot we would be staring at the side of a building – or more properly, at the side of a building-sized box housing an illuminated and animated display on the Promenade. Instead, we have chosen to take the division between beach and Promenade as the viewpoint. This shows the extent of land gained during the recent development of Blackpool's sea defences between 2007 and 2012. The roadway and hotels are a long way off to our right. A series of steps, the 'Spanish Steps', rather than a wall now take the brunt of the sea's force at high tide, absorbing the force little by little rather than withstanding the full weight of a crashing wave. Headlands break up what had previously been more of a straight line towards the Tower.

ROOM WITH SEA VIEW

A CLOSER LOOK at the hotel gardens is given in this view looking back towards our previous viewpoint. Possibly an out-of-season shot, the beach and Promenade are almost deserted, with just a couple of hardy souls making it as far as the sea's edge. Dating photographs can be fraught with difficulty. However, this postcard was sent through the post in 1905 and cannot have been taken earlier than 1897 – witness the overhead tram-wire fittings on the lamp posts. The tram wires themselves are not evident, but it is entirely possible that they were painted out by the company artist – who again has got the horizon slightly wrong, building a veritable tsunami in danger of swamping the South Pier! The row of benches has plenty of capacity for sore-footed walkers.

IN TODAY'S VIEW the Promenade has elegant grassed areas, for the first time in Blackpool's history. The blank expanse of concrete has been broken up by landscaped garden areas with footpaths dissecting them. The gardens of the hotels, however, have all disappeared, redeveloped to make space for the family car of visitors.

The Edwardian shelters set to either side of each access point to the beach have only disappeared with the recent Promenade development, but happily a collection of them has been saved for posterity and can be found further north, just past the North Pier. Again, in this view it is very obvious how the far end of the South Pier has changed with the disappearance of the theatre and pavilion and the erection of more modern attractions that are designed for the enjoyment of rather fewer people than the end-of-pier shows.

LOOKING SOUTH FROM CENTRAL PIER

LOOKING SOUTH FROM the Central Pier, it can be seen that the idea of headlands curving out towards the sea is not exactly a new idea for the Promenade, though it has been taken considerably further in the twenty-first-century design.

The row of benches along the Promenade has been moved to the sea-wall railings. The beach is reasonably well populated and there are crowds walking along the Promenade or riding on the toast-rack tram on the left of the photograph.

Just left of centre, The Manchester pub marks the start of Lytham Road, which stretches from here all the way to Squires Gate Lane. The hotel terraces have mostly given up their gardens. Motor cars are still noticeably absent! Further to the left, the low two-storey building is the Foxhall, one of Blackpool's very early historic houses.

THE MOST NOTICEABLE difference is, of course, the new Promenade. The beach seldom gets crowded in these days of computers and games machines, and buckets and spades no longer feature quite as prominently in Blackpool's shops.

Both The Manchester pub and the Foxhall have been extensively refurbished. The Foxhall, originally built in the late 1600s by the Royalist Tyldesley family as their home, made the transition to a drinking establishment in the early days of Blackpool's popularity.

The Carousel arcade marks the start of the Golden Mile, which stretches north along the Promenade from this point.

Early in the season, the carriages of the pier's Ferris Wheel have been removed and are being checked and cleaned before it starts carrying passengers.

THE CENTRAL PIER ENTRANCE

IN THE EARLY days of seaside piers, the novelty of being able to walk over the water was the pulling power, rather than the shops, bars or amusements to be found on them. Customers paid to go onto the piers (this one with an upper-floor balcony), and in this view of the Central Pier in the Edwardian days the turnstiles are clearly seen on the right, whilst a gate, guarded by attendants,

allows women with perambulators to go through. One such lady seems to be able to resist the attractions of the pier. Her pram seems to be built on the penny-farthing basis, with two huge wheels and one small one at the front.

CENTRAL PIER TODAY. During the 1960s the piers were becoming less popular as other distractions proved more alluring and both the South and Central Piers built large amusement arcades at the entrance to the pier. The North Pier held out a little longer before it did the same.

The entrances to the actual pier are now much less noticeable – they are beneath the billboards at either side of the arcade building. Indeed, from this angle it is impossible to tell that there is a pier behind the building. The pier is now home to a Ferris or 'Big' Wheel which has become an icon of Blackpool in recent years.

The theatre at the end of the pier hosts a show of tribute acts to the likes of Elvis, Buddy and Madonna.

ON THE CENTRAL PIER

THE CENTRAL PIER was especially known in its early days for outdoor dancing. Later, sideshows and games stalls started to spring up along its length.

Along the side of the pier are adverts for patent medicines. Was 'Daisy' a person or a product? '*Kaputine*', advertised further down the pier's side, was sold 'over the counter' in chemists, with no need for a doctor's prescription, and claimed on the packet to cure headaches, influenza and neuralgia (whilst in smaller letters it mentioned such ailments as rheumatism, sciatica, gout, toothache and sleeplessness, in an attempt to convince everyone that it had something to offer them).

THE FERRIS WHEEL on the pier has become as well known a Blackpool landmark as the Tower that we shall soon come to. It started life in 1990, requiring the pier structure to be strengthened to bear its weight. Taken on the same day as the view a couple of pages before, it is waiting for the carriages to be replaced.

The theatre at the end of the pier has risen from the ashes of its predecessors. After the big-name variety shows of the 1950s and '60s, it had a spell as an olde-time music hall, with Linda, one of Blackpool's Nolan Sisters, playing the role of Maggie May for over ten years and 1,000 performances.

The product advertisements have disappeared from the pier's sides and fairground rides (apart from the Big Wheel) have replaced many of the darts, hoop-la and rifle-shooting stalls.

THE GOLDEN MILE

THIS MUST BE the most photographed view of Blackpool. From the Central Pier towards the Tower stretches the glitter and glamour of the Golden Mile. However, in the first years of the twentieth century the arcades have still to move in to replace the hotels. The sea wall is a sloping fence with a few sets of inadequate posts to stop the sea from washing over the Promenade and road at high tide.

In the absence of penny slots, the amusement is provided by donkey rides and orators and peddlers, around whom little crowds have gathered on the beach. The council were soon to pass bylaws banning the latter pair from the beach.

On the roof of a building near the town centre a sign reads 'Coffee Palace' – the Temperance movement's alternative to the ale houses and pubs.

THE CHARACTER OF the Golden Mile changed the most during the late 1970s and '80s when the almost shanty-style extensions of the one-time hotels were wiped away and new, purpose-built large amusement arcades started to be built.

The simple mechanical Edwardian penny-slot machines were made obsolete by electricity. Pinball machines have come and gone and the early video tennis game has evolved into shooting and fighting simulators where a good memory of past sequences, rather than skills and knowledge of the laws of physics, is what is required to win.

A decline in the popularity of amusement machines (we now all have computers and games machines at home) have seen some buildings converted into markets and large attractions such as the Sea Life Centre.

The giant black 'seed pods' sway in the wind – of which there is plenty to be had!

APPROACHING
THE NORTH PIER

IN THE 1930s Blackpool underwent a period of redevelopment. Many new buildings were finished with bright cream tiling like the Information Building on the Promenade. The Information Building fell victim to the latest Promenade developments, but there are plenty of examples to be seen still: the Olympia, the first amusement arcade on the Golden Mile stretch,

and the old Odeon cinema (now Funny Girls), along with several other town-centre buildings.

Blackpool at this time was replacing its trams. The new 'boat' trams replaced the open-air toast-racks and were shortly followed by the double-decked 'balloon' trams and single-decked 'rail-coaches'. The latter lasted until 2012.

THE NEW INFORMATION Building is a stunning piece of architecture, but too new – and perhaps too radical – to be to everyone's taste. The information desk is on the ground floor, with a wedding chapel above it. The registrar conducts marriages in the room with the single window at the end – which, for the assembled witnesses, frames the happy couple against a view of Blackpool Tower.

The Comedy Carpet is a large area filled with catchphrases and sketches from our best-loved comedians from the days of music hall to the twenty-first century. There is something to recognise and chuckle over, no matter how old you are. Entirely free to walk around, it is a great place to be as the sound of people laughing fills the air.

THE TOWER AND PROMENADE

BLACKPOOL TOWER OPENED in May 1894 and was an instant success. Made practical by the invention of lifts and inspired by Paris's Eiffel Tower, Blackpool only built half as high, but with just as much – if not more – foresight. The Parisian tower is just a tower, but the Blackpool one had a circus ring built between the legs and then a sumptuous building that incorporated the tanks from the aquarium that previously occupied the site in a suitably gloomy cavern on the ground floor. An ostentatious ballroom with sprung flooring to take the hundreds of hobnailed boots made Blackpool Tower a hit in sunshine ... and a haven in wet weather!

Note that the Promenade at the time was supported by stilts from the sloping sea wall.

THE TOWER MAY look pretty much the same from outside – it is even having its original Victorian entrance restored – but it has been subject to much change inside. The old fish tanks on the ground floor lasted 110 years but have now been replaced by the Blackpool Tower Dungeon, a depiction of ancient justice, torture and witch hunting. The old menagerie on the top floor where young Albert poked the lion with his stick disappeared long ago. Children's playgrounds, roof gardens complete with flamingos and other delights have at various times come and gone.

The ballroom still draws people to listen to the mighty Wurlitzer organ and the lifts to the top of the Tower go faster these days. You can stand on glass at the top to look vertically down past your feet if you so desire.

TALBOT SQUARE AND
THE TOWN HALL

TALBOT SQUARE, OPPOSITE the North Pier, can be considered the centre of Blackpool. The expansion of Blackpool in the eighteenth and nineteenth centuries grew outwards along the seafront and inland from this point. The Town Hall is centre stage, whilst an island splits the east and west-bound traffic and hosts an ornate drinking fountain.

The tram heads off away from the seafront on the Marton route which will take it around the town. Apart from serving the needs of Blackpool residents, this was also the start and end

of a popular 'Circular Tour' tram ride. We'll take this opportunity now to take a break from the seafront to have a look around the town away from the Promenade before, like the Circular Tour, returning to this point to continue our journey north.

THE TRAM LINES have, since the 1960s, disappeared but there are plans to reintroduce trams to the Square as a proposed line will take them to the railway station on Talbot Road. For many years traffic has passed either side of a large central island. The drinking fountain disappeared long ago and the underground public toilets, the sole surviving of several examples along the Promenade, were closed several years ago. The pavement on the south side of the square has been extended onto the island. In our photograph the road marking is still underway and the road closed to west-bound traffic.

Opposite the Town Hall, an empty site awaits development following a fire in 2009 that destroyed one of Blackpool's early entertainment complexes. It had ended its life as Yates's Wine Lodge and Tivoli Cinema and included a shopping arcade.

GREAT MARTON
POST OFFICE

THE CIRCULAR TOUR trams took visitors on a sightseeing journey through the town, heading down the Promenade from Talbot Square to the South Pier then turning off up Station Road to Lytham Road, where they turned left to the Royal Oak on the corner of Lytham Road and Waterloo Road. Turning east up Waterloo Road, the trams passed the post office at Great Marton, shown

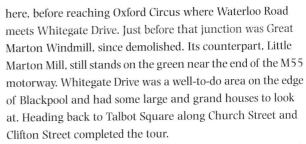

here, before reaching Oxford Circus where Waterloo Road meets Whitegate Drive. Just before that junction was Great Marton Windmill, since demolished. Its counterpart, Little Marton Mill, still stands on the green near the end of the M55 motorway. Whitegate Drive was a well-to-do area on the edge of Blackpool and had some large and grand houses to look at. Heading back to Talbot Square along Church Street and Clifton Street completed the tour.

WHILST NOT ONE of Blackpool's most important buildings, this gives us a chance to compare what has happened to homes over the last century. Other buildings around the group mean it is not as isolated. The number of chimneys has gone down as central heating replaced coal fires. The ivy has been stripped off the walls and the cottages have been stuccoed, perhaps hiding cracks in the brickwork such as is apparent in the shop below the upper window. Satellite dishes and burglar alarm boxes have taken the place of the ivy. The sash windows have been replaced with double glazing and whilst the tram lines have gone, telephone wiring has been added to the scene. And in a typically modern way, gardens have given way to concreted car parking spaces.

WHITEGATE DRIVE –
THE NORTH-SOUTH ARTERY

THE CIRCULAR TOUR used the open-air 'toast-rack' trams. It's easy to see how these trams earned their name, with the lack of sides and the rows of seats. They held up to seventy-four passengers, sixty-nine seated and five standing at the rear. The conductor had to hang on grimly whilst taking care of a money bag and a ticket machine to take fares along the rows of seats!

The trams used to stop on Whitegate Drive to allow a photographer to take a photograph, copies of which would be offered for sale to passengers. Often passengers would have to stand

whilst the seat backs were swung over; they would then sit for the camera facing the sun. The process would then be repeated so they could sit forward again to complete the rest of the tour.

WHITEGATE DRIVE WAS, and remains, one of Blackpool's most important routes north-south away from the Promenade. It had the town hospital, shops for the housing on both sides, and some grand houses of its own along its length. The hospital moved to the present Victoria Hospital, on the far side of the town's municipal Stanley Park, as more ward space became necessary. Whitegate Drive still hosts a large medical centre, and whilst many of the grand houses have been split into multiple occupancy flats, there are many others housing departments of the local authority.

The tram route was closed in the early 1960s. A tourist tour of the town has been made available in recent years by double-decker buses.

STANLEY PARK'S
ITALIAN GARDEN

STANLEY PARK IS Blackpool's big municipal park. Opened in 1926 by the 17th Earl of Derby, it was named after his father, Frederick Stanley, the 16th Earl, who had been the first Member of Parliament for the Blackpool Constituency.

At the centre of the park is the Italian Garden, shown here with a central pond with fountains. This isn't in fact the park's lake as the postcard caption suggests, so we shall see

that on the next page. This is an early view of the garden. There are, as yet, no benches to sit on and little foliage around the ornate screens surrounding the garden, so that the view is uninterrupted to the horizon. The lack of seating does not seem to have deterred the visitors.

THE FOLIAGE HAS matured and grown to block the view to the horizon. At the top of the steps to the left the Pavilion has been built, housing a cafeteria and ice-cream outlet. The gardens have been little changed and the central pond still draws onlookers in summer with its fountains.

The surrounding screens are much as they were, though a larger space between them has been created to open up the vista of the park lake to the east. The park remains as popular as ever with both visitors and residents of Blackpool. A warm weekend can leave families searching for a large enough patch of grass to sit on, whilst concessions to a more modern way of life include areas for skateboarding and mountain biking with ramps, jumps and curved walls to climb.

STANLEY PARK LAKE

THE PARK HAS a large lake that attracts various birds, including ducks and swans, all forever eager for a chunk of bread to be thrown their way. The lake is large enough to contain a couple of islands that are off-limits to boaters, being wildlife reserves. Produced in the early days of the park, this postcard shows a canoe with two intrepid and paddle-wielding passengers; towards the right we can see a more traditional rowboat and the lake's launch, which was for less energetic visitors.

There is a healthy queue at the ticket office for boats and a couple of benches on the jetty for those waiting for their turn, heralded by a shout of 'Come in Number Nine! Your time is up!'

AGAIN, THE MOST significant change is the growth of trees and foliage, blocking the line of sight. The small hut has been replaced by a slightly larger one, though the small one still exists and is just out of shot to the right. The rowing boats and canoes have given way to motor boats and pedal boats and a large launch operates on the lake in summer – another seldom recognised bit of Blackpool history, as it is an old Blackpool lifeboat given an extension of life!

The birdlife using the lake is as prolific as ever and there is a large colony of herons that build the most ungainly looking nests in the trees on the northern edge of the lake where it is a little quieter.

LAYTON

THIS IS WESTCLIFFE DRIVE, Layton, seen in 1924. The village of Layton has been swallowed up by Blackpool but existed long before Blackpool – or seaside resorts in general – were ever thought of. The modern district stretches from the boundary with Bispham to the north, where Layton's railway station can be found, to Marton in the south; from Warbreck to the west to Grange Park to the east.

In 1066 it was held by Tostig, the brother of King Harold. In 1257 Henry III granted the Botiller family (later Butler) the right to hold a weekly market and a three-day annual fair. But men had lived here much earlier – witness the arrowheads found in 1970 within the skeleton of an elk dating from 11,000 years ago.

By 1924, though, Westcliffe Drive was a shopping street with buildings that are easily recognisable today.

THE DRIVE IS a major route into Blackpool, particularly from the north. The M55 motorway in the 1970s provided an alternative route but visitors from the north would normally leave the motorway before reaching that more southerly route.

In the past few years the roadway has been divided, with benches provided for those who like to breathe exhaust fumes. The row of shops still exists, though it houses fewer shops these days as Costcutter occupies three units and the pharmacy takes two. The bungalow at the end of the row has gone, and a two-storey building has taken its place. Further to the left the houses still stand. The Layton Institute, standing out of sight over the road on the left, is one of a few large Blackpool clubs, and is noted for good entertainment.

ADELAIDE STREET

ADELAIDE STREET RUNS downhill
to the sea at the back of the Winter
Gardens. In this view there are still
evidence of gardens, though some of the
green space has been given over to the
Big Wheel, a giant Ferris Wheel: it was
220ft high, with thirty carriages (each
capable of accommodating over thirty
passengers). Built in 1896, two years
after the Tower opened and only half the
Tower's height, the wheel was an instant
disaster. It took half an hour to revolve,
by which time passengers were twiddling
their thumbs and bored. Not even the
installation of a table-tennis table in one
of the carriages was enough to save it,
though it remained until 1928 before
being broken up, the carriages sold off.
One still survives in the countryside
several miles away.

THE SPACE LEFT by the Big Wheel's demolition was built over in the 1930s when the Olympia exhibition hall was added to the Winter Gardens. This unfortunately blocked any external views of the beautiful Horseshoe Pavilion and did away with the garden part of the Winter Gardens. The Olympia and side entrance of the Winter Gardens were faced with ivory tiles, along with many other buildings at the time. For a period the Olympia housed an indoor amusements arcade complete with large fairground rides.

The Houndshill shopping centre development of the 1980s required Adelaide Street to be divided, and there is now no clear view down to the sea. The hotels on the left of the road all survive but in the last year buildings have been cleared on the right-hand side to make room for another car park.

VICTORIA STREET

THIS IS ONE of the oldest photographs in this collection. It shows Victoria Street in the 1860s, looking east, from a few yards distance from the seafront. The Crystal Palace building, originally the Victoria Terrace, with its impressive veranda, was an early shopping, library, lecture-hall and meeting-room complex. It was the first of Blackpool's places of entertainment (other than drinking establishments), and readings by local officials and clergy were particularly popular.

William Pearson's shop on the corner displays glass, china and earthenware goods in the window. The house at the top of the street is 'Bank Hey', the home of Dr John Cocker – whose son, William Henry Cocker, would become Blackpool's first mayor. Some idea of the extent of

Blackpool's development at the time is gleaned from the empty horizon behind the house to the right.

THE WINTER GARDENS now occupies the site of Bank Hey at the top of the street. We shall see more of them on the next page.

Both Victoria Street and Bank Hey Street (running left to right across the foreground) are pedestrianised today. Goldsmiths' shop, despite being a modern development, has many deliberate echoes of the old Victoria Terrace in its chamfered corner and the dividing pilasters or flattened columns of the upper storey.

Victoria Street was extensively redeveloped in the early 1980s with the development of the Houndshill shopping centre to the north and south – whose buildings, with the pedestrianisation, now extend out over what had been the old pavement, considerably narrowing the street.

THE WINTER GARDENS

THIS IMAGE IS from several years after the photograph on the previous page but, whilst taken from further up Victoria Street, is essentially the same view. The house, Bank Hey, was offered by Dr W.H. Banks as the site for a proposed Winter Gardens. The purchase of the house and land, whilst being superbly placed for the purpose, was so expensive that a stipulation was made to the architects that the house had to be incorporated, rather than demolished and built over. Its walls can still be seen from inside the modern-day Olympia complex, which was built in 1929 on the site of the Big Wheel, seen in this view dominating the skyline to the right. At the time, hotels, shops and a church occupied the top of Victoria Street.

APART FROM THE Winter Gardens themselves, all of the buildings shown in the earlier photograph have disappeared to make way for the modern-day shopping street that Victoria Street has become.

The Houndshill development, on the southern side of the street to our right, has extended up to the top of the street with a glass canopy forming a sheltering arcade along the shop fronts. The narrowing of the street caused by the building of both this and the properties on the northern side has led to the partial obscuring of the Winter Gardens' Coronation Street entrance. In the 1930s the building was resurfaced in the creamy white tiles that covered many of Blackpool's buildings at that time.

ST JOHN'S
PARISH CHURCH

THESE DAYS CONSIDERED the centre of Blackpool, St John's Square is a bustling place surrounded by shops. Our photograph shows the same recognisable church standing within its own railed church ground and graveyard. Even so, the amount of space in the graveyard is limited and by 1873 a new cemetery had been opened at Layton to take all further burials.

The present church of 1878 replaced a smaller brick one of 1821, which itself had been enlarged three times in its short history. As St John's Square changed in nature and became

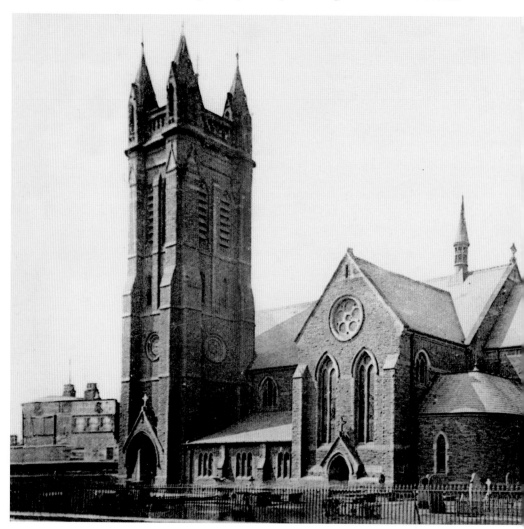

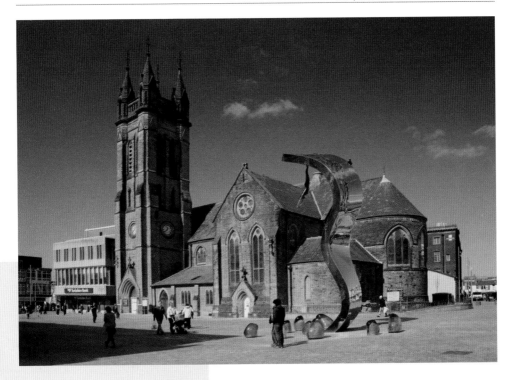

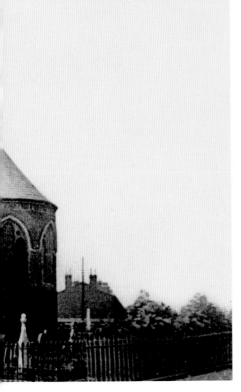

busier, most of the burials were removed to Layton and the area in front of the church incorporated into the Square with a small amount of landscaping. In a recent redevelopment, the remaining graves and grassed areas have been removed also.

WHAT A DIFFERENCE! The graveyard and railings have gone and the roadway has all but disappeared, with the Square now being pedestrianized. It had originally been going to be open to buses, but the public liked the traffic-free environment and so the bus shelters have been used instead to store bicycles for hire.

A large modern sculpture dominates the open space and nearby cafés place tables and chairs outdoors to give the Square a Continental feel. This, on a blustery day, requires a little imagination and not a little stamina and determination on the part of the diner...

The Yorkshire Bank's branch to the left of the church is a side view as the main entrance is on Abingdon Street, round the corner.

ABINGDON STREET
POST OFFICE

ABINGDON STREET IS one of Blackpool's town-centre shopping streets, running north-south from Talbot Road, which leads from the train station to the seafront and on to the impressive front of the Winter Gardens.

Halfway along it is the post office, on this postcard the 'new' general post office. Originally built with a railed area allowing light to the basement rooms, the post office reflects the success of the Royal Mail at the time. Inside, a grand hall with counters the length of the

building allowed for the fast processing of holiday crowds wanting to buy postage stamps as well as locals and businesses who need to send parcels through the post. Peeping over the top can be seen the tower of St John's parish church and on the right a mock half-timbered building housing a motor garage.

THE RAILINGS HAVE gone, and the drop they protected, which gave some daylight to the basement levels, has been backfilled to pavement level and now supports a row of listed old red telephone kiosks. The magnificent building is a post office no more and the long row of counters, through which thousands – if not millions – of stamps have been sold now stand empty, save for two or three where customers queue to pick up packages. The actual post office is now hidden away in the basement of WHSmiths on Bank Hey Street.

The half-timbered building to the right has been a market hall since 1928. Currently being refurbished, the construction work uncovered a door lintel with the words 'police station' deeply engraved in it – the building's original purpose.

NEW PROMENADES

THE ORIGINAL PROMENADE was proving inadequate for the number of tourists flooding into Blackpool. Between 1902 and 1905 the Promenade was widened all the way down from the North Pier to South Shore. The tramway was given its own 'road' alongside that for other traffic and the resulting Promenade would be familiar to anyone who visited Blackpool for the next 100 years. Our postcard clearly shows the amount of land gained at the time.

The large building next to the Tower is the Alhambra of 1899, renamed the Palace in 1904. Apart from the obvious vertical attraction of the Tower, the Alhambra building was very similar, with a theatre, a circus and a ballroom. It was demolished to make way for Lewis's store in the 1960s.

The Lane Ends Hotel, at its side, was one of Blackpool's earliest hotels, advertising in 1786.

THE WORK BEING done in the earlier photograph included the grey cobbled section of sea wall on the left of this present-day view. The grey cobbles extended all the way past the Pleasure Beach to Starr Gate where Blackpool ends and the sand dunes of St Annes take over.

The work extended the land – and therefore the coastline – as the work 100 years later has done again. The rows of four square projections running down the old sea wall are the remains of the wooden piles that held the wooden staircase down to the beach. The modern steps have been in place since 2008, whilst the Promenade was built behind them, and are starting to acquire a colouring given to them by the sea. The Alhambra has gone and so has Lewis's store, which replaced it. The current building housed a Woolworths store, but they too have disappeared from high streets.

THE
NORTH PIER

THE NORTH PIER is the oldest of Blackpool's three piers. Built on a direct line from the train station to the Promenade, it was visible to visitors long before they reached it and was designed so that if people kept on walking they would walk straight onto the pier.

It maintained a certain class: no open-air dancing would be found on the North Pier and the shops sold quality items, including one shop that sold fur coats. Some of these were knocked into the sea with the wrecking of the ship *Sirene* against the pier in 1892. It is understood that several of them were gleefully recovered from the beach once the tide went out...

A T-shaped landing stage was built at the end of the pier and steamer trips used it as a terminus.

IT WAS THE pier that for the longest time held on to its original purpose. The views of the Tower from the North Pier are perhaps the best the town can offer. During the season the benches along its side are still crowded with visitors enjoying the sun or an ice-cream.

Its sun lounge, at the far end, offers music and a sheltered sun trap and the end-of-pier theatre has seen some huge names in its time, including The Beatles and comedy duo Morecambe and Wise.

In the past, a uniformed attendant would take money for a peep down a brass telescope on a tripod and could describe points of interest. A single strip of wood is all that remains of the box where it was kept. It is unrecognisable unless you know what it is.

PRINCESS PARADE

THE POSTCARD WAS labelled 'Princes Parade' but it should actually be the feminine form 'Princess Parade'. This portion of the Promenade was opened in May 1912 by Princess Louise, the Princess Royal, eldest daughter of King Edward VII. An estimated 10,000 light bulbs were festooned along Princess Parade for the opening – the origin of Blackpool Illuminations, as the lights were used again six months later, drawing huge crowds to Blackpool.

Bailey's Metropole Hotel was, and remains, the only hotel to be built west of the Promenade roadway and was one of Blackpool's very first hotels, advertising a year before the Lane Ends Hotel in 1785.

The buildings along the road still have gardens at the front at this time, leaving vehicles vying for space with the trams heading north towards the Gynn and Fleetwood.

BAILEY'S METROPOLE RETAINS the second part of the name and has spent a while in the ownership of Butlin's, the holiday camp people. The gardens have been stripped from the opposite buildings in order to widen the road – which, for a long time, remained the only part of Blackpool's tram tracks to share space with road traffic. With the latest Promenade developments they are now segregated. Platforms have been built to allow passengers ready access to the new trams introduced in April 2012.

The most obvious changes are the large multi-storey apartment block at the corner, past the Metropole and the cenotaph, of which more on the next page. There is a collection of Edwardian shelters on the Promenade which have been moved from further south with the seafront developments.

PRINCESS GARDENS,
THE MEMORIAL GARDENS

PRINCESS GARDENS IS one of a pair, the other being at the far end of the Metropole Hotel. In this view the gardens are well favoured by tourists, who are taking in the sun in thick coats, hats, suits and waistcoats. They have all decided that the sign declaring 'please keep off the grass' refers only to the lawn in the centre.

A flagpole is the centrepiece of the garden. Facing us is the Clifton Hotel, yet another of Blackpool's very early hotels. A Dreadnought tram heads north from Talbot Square and the

North Pier. Whilst the overhead tram wires are in place, the tram does not seem to have a pole in place to touch them, which could date the photograph to 1897 (even though the postcard was postmarked in 1915).

TODAY IT IS a Garden of Remembrance. The elegant monument has scenes of First World War battles sculpted from the iron of melted cannons. More modern additions contain the names of Blackpool's heroes who gave their lives in more recent conflicts. Wreathes are often to be seen resting against the memorial and ceremonies are held there on Remembrance Sunday.

The Clifton Hotel in the background looks little changed on the outside – the inside is likely to have changed considerably! It is now operated by the Travelodge hotel chain.

Some of the buildings on the left of the photograph have changed considerably too. The large brick building was built as a four-screen cinema but is currently unused. Next to it is a Chinese restaurant and the bank on the corner is a public house appropriately called The Counting House.

LOOKING NORTH

IN THIS PHOTOGRAPH, taken before the construction of Princess Parade, there is no colonnade around the Metropole Hotel, which has yet to build a conservatory around the front entrance. Posted in 1903, this postcard shows the sea wall sloping down sharply to the beach from a narrow Promenade, supported from the sloping sea wall by struts or columns.

The beach has a number of bathing huts. These were available to bathers and would be manhandled or drawn by horses to the water's edge to allow for modest bathing. Males and females were kept strictly apart by having time slots allocated to each sex.

Looking northwards, the coast turns sharply inwards at the Gynn and Promenades on three levels have been constructed to join them. The sender of this postcard describes this as a 'favourite spot at moonlight'. Whilst scenery may change, other things remain constant!

AGAIN THE RECENT Promenade and sea-defences developments have extended the land out to sea (when the tide is in!) or on to the beach. Some of the Edwardian shelters from the older Promenade farther south have been gathered here in a row of nostalgia with a practical purpose. The Promenade may well have had a lot of money spent on it, but that hasn't made much difference to the winds coming off the Irish Sea!

Blackpool starts to get a little quieter as we head north from this point. The hotels tend to be a bit larger and put on entertainment for their guests and there are fewer independent attractions – no fairgrounds, no rides, no kiss-me-quick hat stalls or ice-cream vendors.

THE NORTH PROMENADE

A VERY EARLY Victorian-era view of North Promenade. At this period there is a slade down from the Promenade level to the beach. As the land begins to rise, the Promenade development has led to two levels – an upper and middle Promenade.

A row of horse-drawn bathing machines are parked opposite a number of rowing boats. Day trippers are sitting or walking on the beach, many utilising the slope of the cobbled sea wall as a support.

The tide has just gone out – witness the darker wet sand that is still not far from the slade. Also, the fact that the bathing machines are not in use is probably an indication that it's not too long since the sea was covering the beach.

THE SAME SPOT today is a little more developed. The Promenade now curves round from in front of the Metropole Hotel behind us and the slope of the Promenade leads not to the beach, but will shortly level out before climbing again towards the North Pier. The stepped slope provides seating in warm weather, but this is no longer a popular part of the beach for holidaymakers – even when the tide is out.

The terraced row of hotels still exists, the original ground-floor frontages hidden by sun lounges added as extensions to the hotels. There is a noticeable lack of chimneys on today's roofline! The silver-painted railings are the last surviving example of the style of railings that used to extend all the way to South Shore.

THE CLAREMONT HOTEL

THE CLAREMONT HOTEL, Queen's Promenade, a well-to-do spot. By the time that Blackpool had started to grow, and with the arrival of attractions like the Pleasure Beach, the North Shore area was deemed to be a little quieter. Taken in the days when there were less than 100 telephone numbers in Blackpool, the short-term residents of the Claremont are taking their ease in the gardens, segregated from passers-by on the pavement by heavy iron railings. As a sign of advancing times, two motor cars are parked in front of the hotel (whose curtains have all been drawn and then draped just so for the photographer).

Many of the large hotels grew by buying up adjoining properties and knocking through internal walls on the ground floor. Steps still lead to what used to be other front-door entrances.

THE IRON RAILINGS are long gone, and the gardens with them, as the number of motor cars requiring parking space has gone up from the two cars in the previous photograph. The ground-floor extension, as with many other hotels, has been built onto the external walls (which have been converted to an internal wall and wallpapered).

The standard of hotel accommodation has improved dramatically in the last century. Hotels no longer boast of 'hot running water' or even 'colour television lounge'. Some of Blackpool's older hotel traditions – sharing rooms (and even beds) with strangers, expecting visitors to provide their own food which would then be cooked by the hotel 'chef', the midnight dash down the corridor to use the WC and having a contraption on the table containing stale beer to trap flies – have all disappeared!

THE FLAGSHIP HOTELS

THE NUMBER OF hotels offering accommodation of high quality has grown considerably, but the Imperial has always been something of a flagship on Blackpool's Promenade. Opened in 1867, the roll call of visitors reads something like a 'Who's Who'.

In the middle of the stretch of cliffs from the North Pier to the Gynn, the views across the sea are uninterrupted. On clear days it is possible to see the mountains of the Lake District and the Barrow peninsular. On exceptionally clear days you can see the hills of the Isle of Man.

Built to impress, the hotel was set further back from the road than other hotels and had larger gardens to the front. Running alongside the road, the pavement is edged with railings with a strip of grass before the cliff falls to the sea wall.

THE IMPERIAL HOTEL of today has changed hands a few times and is currently run by the Puma group. Whilst more modern, purpose-built hotels have appeared in Blackpool, the Imperial has always retained its place in both local and national eyes as an important and prestigious hotel.

Numerous Prime Ministers and Cabinet members have stayed there during their party's annual convention. One bar is named Thatcher's Bar and there are photographs of many familiar and historic faces on the walls.

During a particularly difficult time – for a short while, following the bombing of a hotel in Brighton, there was perceived to be a high risk of terrorist attack during conventions – it was guarded by a Royal Navy submarine off the shore of Blackpool!

THE MIDDLE WALK

LABELLED 'CENTRAL PROMENADE' on this postcard, postmarked 1923, this is today's Middle Walk, looking south towards the Tower and North Pier from a point close to the Gynn.

When first constructed, the three Promenades had a series of sloping paths leading from the upper to the middle Promenade. At this stage at least one Edwardian shelter occupies the roadway in the middle distance, opposite the Imperial Hotel.

Note the fine tram shelter on the main or upper Promenade towards the left of the photograph. In the distance, on the beach, the sands look as though there are a substantial number of people this side of the North Pier.

THE CONSTRUCTION OF a separate roadway to take the trams off the road required the widening of the Promenade – a little difficult at the point where the cliffs fall away. It has been done by building colonnades along the Middle Walk and the footpath above is supported by the colonnades. They were completed in 1925.

The Middle Walk annually hosts a number of events. The roadway is easily closed without affecting the town's traffic and is therefore a safe place to host vehicle rallies, the start and finish points for walking or running events and visiting stages of national or international events such as cycle racing.

Otherwise it provides a haven of peace and quiet on days when there are no events on, and people can walk or sit and watch the sea with little to disturb them.

THE GYNN

AT THE GYNN is a natural rent in the cliffs where the slade ran down to the beach. The Promenade makes an acute curve inwards at this point and then heads north once again. The Gynn Inn was a well-established calling place here; references to the inn exist from around 1700. In the 1840s the innkeeper had arranged horse racing on the sands at the Gynn, plus donkey racing, trotting and a sack race.

At this early stage the tram tracks had to follow the curve round, the large Dreadnoughts having to slow right down to negotiate the steep curve. Later, the worst of the curve was made less steep

and the trams were then able to do a more graceful 'S' bend to carry on north along the cliffs towards Bispham.

TODAY THE HOTELS stretch all the way around the bend but the junction of the Promenade road with Queen's Promenade is now governed by a roundabout. Previously the Promenade curved to head inland up Warbreck Hill Road and Queen's Promenade was joined on at right angles. Blackpool's trams stopped here and those of the Blackpool and Fleetwood Tram Co. had to be used to travel further north until both companies merged. With the merger, the tracks north and south were joined and the rent in the cliffs filled in enough to allow for a gentler curve. The old Gynn Inn had to go, and today's Gynn pub stands at the end of Dickson Road just before the roundabout.

THE PUTTING GREENS,
THE GYNN

AT THE BACK of Dickson Road's northern end is a large garden with a putting green. Putting was an extremely popular sport in parks and gardens in towns all over the UK. It started at St Andrews golf course in Scotland in the 1860s, where an eighteen-hole set of putting greens was created for women, for whom the energetic action of swinging a golf club was deemed unseemly.

Our view looks north-west over the gardens, from the corner of Seafield Road and Finchley Road, towards the Savoy Hotel in the centre of the photograph. The flag mast in the gardens across Warbreck Hill Road is one of several that we have seen along the Promenade on our journey south

to north. The gardens are fenced and the fence posts buttressed against the winds that regularly blows off the sea.

THIS WOULD APPEAR to be one of the least changed views in our collection. The garden fencing has disappeared, to be replaced by railings, and the putting greens are less in evidence, though the concrete slabs marking the tee spots are still there. Just out of view to the left, a crazy-golf course has been created, perhaps taking custom from the putting greens.

The Savoy Hotel looks much the same as it does in the earlier photograph, although a couple of the hotels behind it have swapped gables for loft conversions that give them extra letting rooms. However, the grand flag mast has gone, to be replaced by a much inferior and hardly noticeable affair. The bottom portion of the gardens across Warbreck Hill Road, towards the Promenade, is now a car and coach park.

THE CLIFFS AND
QUEEN'S PROMENADE

A VIEW OF the Promenade looking north from Gynn Square. In this early view there is little development apart from an apartment block between the Savoy and the top of the hill, though there are some houses behind the Savoy; many of these seem to be residential, but some were let to visitors as guest houses. The cliffs continue to rise in height and – apart from a short landscaped portion at the Gynn – have been left to their own devices, being scrub grass with little to prevent them from being eroded by the sea.

The Savoy Hydro Hotel is the only large hotel on this stretch. Despite being built of brick, without even the later addition of the cream-tiled ground-floor terrace extension on its side, the artist has left the hotel uncoloured, preferring to let the original black and white photograph underneath show.

THERE ARE NO gaps now along the Queen's Promenade, as the roadway has grandly become. The royal connection is maintained in the first few side streets: King George Avenue, King Edward Avenue and Empress Drive.

The Cliffs Hotel is an impressive pile, competing with the Savoy in similar brick and with stone decoration and a low dome. It sits above the curve in the tram track, which now carries on to Fleetwood. The trams of the Blackpool and Fleetwood Co. ran between the Gynn and Fleetwood and also up Dickson Road to Blackpool North railway station.

The road junction now has a roundabout and the new building on the left is an electric sub-station. The gardens behind it are still there, and on a summer's evening wild rabbits often sit out on the grass.

UNCLE TOM'S CABIN

OPENED IN THE 1860s, Uncle Tom's Cabin was a frequent destination that took in a walk along the cliffs. We are just about in Bispham – and indeed Uncle Tom's Cabin has been called Bispham's first place of entertainment. Bars, meetings, entertainment, 'American' portaits taken and finished while you wait... The figures on the roof portray the characters of Harriet Beecher Stowe's 1852 anti-slavery novel of the same name.

Set at an angle to the cliffs and therefore to the road, the collection of buildings here, at one time set far from the cliff edge, fell (literally) prey to the erosion of the cliff which eventually undermined the corner of the building, causing the windows to start dropping out and the collapse of the structure.

THIS IS THE only photograph pairing not to match. The original Uncle Tom's Cabin having fallen over the cliff, there was some obvious reluctance to build a replacement on the edge of the cliff again. The structure that survives today was built well away from the precipice, on the opposite side of the coastal roadway.

From being one of Blackpool's few places of entertainment, Uncle Tom's Cabin has a lot of competition in the town today. Many of the hotels close by – which didn't even exist when the original cabin was built – now book cabaret entertainment for their guests each night. Uncle Tom's Cabin is a pub and has rooms to book for special events.

THE CLIFFS AND BOATING POOL

THE EROSION OF the cliffs was checked by extending the sea wall northwards. Where the cliffs emerge from the Promenade, the first few feet have been encased in concrete, creating a rockery with seating from which the grassy slope rises to the top of the cliffs.

The viewpoint is just a little north of the present Uncle Tom's Cabin. At this point a boating pool has been created with 'speed boats' for hire; the pond is divided and rowing boats occupy the portion closest to the sea. The tower structure contains a lift from the top to the bottom of the cliff. As the crowds show, to be here on a summer's day is a pleasant way to spend your time!

FURTHER EROSION HAS led to the removal of some of the grassy slope, now replaced with large slabs of stone. The slabs that marked the edges of the path have been given a coat of concrete but the big differences here are the changes to the attractions.

The lift ceased to operate many years ago and despite almost constant lobbying by nearby residents and hotel owners has remained closed. The elegant arch has gone and the enclosed bridge, a shelter for those waiting to descend, is enclosed no more.

The boating pool has been emptied of water, filled with tyres and is now a go-kart track. Whilst the photograph was taken out of season, it is probably true to say that these days the area seldom attracts the crowds shown in the earlier photograph.

FOOTPATHS, SHELTERS AND CYCLEWAYS

THIS VIEW DATES from the 1930s and shows the cliff tops close to the site of the Miners' Convalescent Home which sits in extensive (for Blackpool seafront!) grounds behind the gap in buildings to the right of the photograph.

The building at the far end of the path on the horizon is Bispham Station – for trams, not trains – and the pathway is well away from the cliff edge, so much so that there is no fencing at all, allowing anyone who wants to climb down (or sit on) the steep cliff face full freedom to do so. For the less foolhardy, elegant Edwardian shelters were set in place around 1905 to keep off those sea breezes – winds which regularly reach 50mph or more on the cliffs!

FOR ANYONE WHO thought that the erosion of the cliffs would have been halted by the building of the sea wall, this modern-day view may come as a surprise. To take the photograph from the exact same viewpoint it would have been necessary to float in the air above the current slope of the cliffs!

The 50mph winds reach 70mph in winter, and over time the sand they carry from the beach whittles away at the soil covering – and even at the rock. Modern-day health and safety concerns mean that the cliffs are now fenced, but the cliff has reached the very edge of the path. A second pathway has been added for cyclists, and this is the site of the large tableaux that mark the northern limit of the famous Blackpool Illuminations every autumn.

NORBRECK CLIFFS

THIS IS GETTING close to as far as you can come to the north and still be in Blackpool. Anchorsholme comes after Norbreck and is on the edge of Cleveleys. On Anchorsholme beach are the few remaining timbers of a wrecked barque, *Abana*, which ended its days in a huge storm at Christmas 1894. Just a few yards away, in January 2008, the ferry *Riverdance* came to rest in similar circumstances and had to be scrapped, cut up and removed from the beach.

Here at Norbreck, the long string of hotels from Blackpool has yet to reach this far north. There appears to be no man-made sea defences or Promenade and the cliffs look more like sand dunes with the start of a covering of grass. A well-defined pathway leads down to the beach.

THE LINE OF hotels from Blackpool has now reached Norbreck! The tramway has been fenced for safety as the trams can move fairly quickly along the coast at this point having left behind the crowded Promenade of Blackpool. The new fleet of Flexity2 trams coming into service in 2012 are faster than the trams Blackpool has been used to for well over 100 years.

The pathway leading down is still there and now covered with tarmac. It leads down to a Promenade and wall that protect the cliffs from further erosion by the sea. The cliffs themselves now have a well-established covering of grass and a good crop of dandelions adding a sprinkling of yellow to the ground close to the camera!

NORBRECK CASTLE

TO THE NORTH of the junction of Norbreck
Road with the Promenade is the Norbreck
Castle. Whilst it is a grand name, this is
no ancient fortress, home of lords from
long ago. It is a hotel, built with a row of
crenulations on the top to resemble a castle.
In fact, in this early photograph of the hotel
the name on the gable end is 'Norbreck Hall',
a name dwarfed by the large letters spelling
out 'Private Hotel'.

With its crenulated tower and cluster of
other buildings, including a mock Tudor
black-and-white hall, it looks every inch
the castle that it's not. On the left of the
photograph, a flagpole stands on the lawn.
However, no flag is flying – so perhaps the
lord and his lady are not at home.

TODAY THE NORBRECK Castle would indeed do justice to a lord and lady. Several decades of development can be seen, and whilst the mock Tudor hall has disappeared, the castle motif of crenulations has been added to each new building project as it has come along. The latest and largest addition has soaring towers in contrasting colours. The hotel boasts one of the biggest car parks for visitors of any hotel in Blackpool.

Conventions, concerts, antiques shows, postcard fairs, film-related and other one-off events are featured throughout the year at the Norbreck.

The house on the right has had new windows fitted, but the old windows from the previous photograph, with their many small panes of glass, do look quite attractive.

BISPHAM VILLAGE

BISPHAM WAS MENTIONED in the Domesday Book and so pre-dates Blackpool considerably. The church has Norman stones in the doorway, though they have been re-cut. Red Bank Road leads down from the seafront at the point where the autumn Illuminations finish (or start, depending on the way you move through them!).

On the right is Ivy Cottage, a venerable old house of cruck construction which operated as a café and was much loved by visitors. At the crossroads, in the middle distance, Devonshire Road

crosses Blackpool to the left and Cleveleys and Fleetwood to the right. The terraced rows of houses are on the continuation of Red Bank Road which climbs up a hill to arrive on top of the cliffs at the sea.

IT'S ALMOST IMPOSSIBLE to recognise this view as the same spot. The white building on the left and the terraced row across Devonshire Road are the only buildings to exist in both photographs. The nearest building on the left is a supermarket and the row after the white building has been demolished to allow for widening of the road as a large roundabout now stands in place of the crossroads.

On the right, Ivy Cottage disappeared in the mid-1950s and modern shops and offices take its place. Its role as a café has been taken over by a chip shop on the corner by the roundabout, a small café at the back of the market and a pizza takeaway opposite.

MORE BISPHAM VILLAGE

SWINGING 90 DEGREES to the right from the previous spread, we see the local bus arriving at the village centre from a very twisting and narrow All Hallows Road. A row of old cottages with tiny windows is to our right, faced with a whitewashed covering.

The village centre has a pleasingly green and natural feel to it, with the trees and the neat garden fenced off in the foreground. On the left is a wall made of duckstones – pebbles the size of a duck's body taken from the beach and cemented together. A lady in a shawl has come out to watch the bus go by – who says that there was no excitement in the old days?!

ONCE AGAIN WE look for a landmark to recognise in the modern view. The layout of All Hallows Road has been quite drastically altered to take out the bend that the bus was navigating in the previous photograph. Apart from two houses behind the trees of the little railed garden, now standing at a seemingly strange angle, this could be a different view altogether.

The old terraced row of tiny cottages with their small windows and miniscule doors have gone, otherwise the three cars to the right would have been parked with their noses against the cottages' walls. There is now a large car park with shops and offices – Bispham Chambers – around it. The current row of shops on the right stands well back from where the road used to run.

ILLUMINATED TRAMS

SINCE THE ILLUMINATIONS started there have been special illuminated tramcars. The first specially built ones were in the form of a lifeboat and a grand gondola. These were replaced by a couple of the old Standard trams, used mainly on the round town routes, which were decked out in light bulbs. One such is seen here. These continued in use through until the 1960s.

Walking through the lights was always made a little more exciting as a young lad when the illuminated trams rumbled by. And taking the two-hour trip up and down the Illuminations by tram just wasn't the same unless your tram was lit up outside too!

At least one of the two former illuminated Standards still exists in a museum, and Standard Tram 147 is often seen on the tracks operating as one of the Blackpool heritage fleet.

IN THE 1960s a number of new illuminated tramcars were built. The Wild West train, with locomotive and a calaboose trailer, came along in 1962 and was a firm favourite with visitors. It was seldom seen other than during the Illuminations but was seen quite often on television as it was sponsored by ATV Television.

There was also a 1950s-styled Rocket with the interior passenger compartment raked up at 20 degrees, a frigate which is still seen running today; other trams included a Mississippi paddle steamer, sold off in the 1980s, and the Hovertram, a double-decked piece of fantasy modelled on a hovercraft. The Western train was refurbished with the help of a hefty Lottery grant and it was hoped that the Rocket could be similarly saved. The illuminated fleet has been joined more recently by a trawler, converted from one of Blackpool's single-deck trams.

If you enjoyed this book, you may also be interested in...

Blackpool

DAVE THOMPSON

Cheerfully unpretentious and brash with all the trimmings one would expect of a traditional seaside resort, Blackpool remains the iconic resort town, but there is more to its richly coloured history than you might think. This absorbing collection of images reveals the changing face of the town during the past century. Over 200 old postcards and photographs help highlight Blackpool's remarkable transformation from a fledgling resort. Aspects of everyday life in the town are featured here, including social occasions, the pleasure steamers that once plied their trade from the piers, seaside entertainment and old cherished street scenes of bygone Blackpool. This book is a valuable pictorial history, which will waken nostalgic memories for some readers, whilst offering a unique glimpse at the past for others.

9780752444949

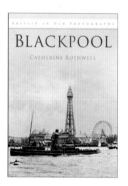

Blackpool in Old Photographs

CATHERINE ROTHWELL

There can be no better example of Victorian enterprise than the amazing success story of Blackpool whose pioneering spirit and bold publicity coupled with diligent application of the town's motto 'Progress' proved it to be true. There were great natural advantages: 7 miles of flat, golden sands washed twice daily by no ordinary sea but 'the bounding main'. With the help of the railways, equally confident and zealous, the workers were speedily brought from sprawling, industrial areas and once in, they were captivated. Here was splendour in buildings and interiors, safe bathing (all the rage), a cornucopia of entertainment and day-long merriment extending into night. The crowds came in their thousands year after year, as children, with their own children, and with their grandchildren, to 'wonderful Blackpool, the most progressive resort under the flag'. This book is a truly wonderful record of the growth of Blackpool into the national treasure it is today.

9780752449500

Haunted Blackpool

STEPHEN MERCER

Blackpool has long been a favourite for holidaymakers and conjures up cosy images of theme parks, donkey rides, candy floss and ice-cream. However, this popular seaside resort also harbours some disturbing secrets. Discover the shadier side of Blackpool with this terrifying collection of true-life tales from across the town. Featuring the ghosts of some of the most iconic buildings, such as Blackpool Tower, the Grand Theatre and Blackpool Opera House, this book is guaranteed to make your blood run cold. Drawing on historical and contemporary sources and containing many tales which have never before been published, *Haunted Blackpool* will delight everyone interested in the paranormal. Read on... if you dare!

9780752460215

Visit our website and discover thousands of other History Press books.

www.thehistorypress.co.uk